GRAND CENTRAL

A BOOK OF POSTCARDS

Pomegranate

SAN FRANCISCO

Pomegranate Communications, Inc.
Box 808022, Petaluma CA 94975
800 227 1428; www.pomegranate.com

Pomegranate Europe Ltd.
Unit 1, Heathcote Business Centre, Hurlbutt Road
Warwick, Warwickshire CV34 6TD, UK
[+44] 0 1926 430111; sales@pomeurope.co.uk

ISBN 978-0-7649-6333-9
Pomegranate Catalog No. AA745

Pomegranate publishes books of postcards on a wide range of subjects.
Please contact the publisher for more information.

Cover designed by Ronni Madrid
Printed in Korea
21 20 19 18 17 16 15 14 13 12   10 9 8 7 6 5 4 3 2 1

To facilitate detachment of the postcards from this book, fold each card along its perforation line before tearing.

The first rail line into New York City began service in 1832. Others soon followed, and by the late 1840s the city held a haphazard, aboveground rail network plagued by complaints about noise, traffic problems, frequent accidents, and pollution from the steam locomotives.

In 1869, shipping magnate Cornelius Vanderbilt purchased property between 42nd and 48th Streets and Lexington and Madison Avenues for construction of a new train depot and rail yard. His $6.4 million "Grand Central Depot" opened in October 1871. This busy station was expanded in 1898 and further renovated in 1900, reopening as "Grand Central Station." The reconfigured depot featured a spectacular glass-and-steel train shed rivaling the Eiffel Tower and Crystal Palace as the nineteenth century's most dramatic engineering achievement. But the age of steam locomotives was ending. A catastrophic train collision in the smoke-filled Park Avenue Tunnel on January 8, 1902, caused a public outcry and increased demand for underground electric trains. Soon plans were afoot to demolish Grand Central Station and create a new electric-train terminal in its place.

This new "Grand Central Terminal" would be expensive. The railroad needed not only to electrify its rails but also carve deep into Manhattan's bedrock. The solution to meeting the projected $80 million budget (roughly $2 billion in today's terms) was ingenious: The area from 45th to 49th Streets was paved over, and real estate developers were sold "air rights" to erect buildings over the concealed tracks. Construction of the new terminal took ten years.

Grand Central Terminal opened to great fanfare on February 2, 1913, and development around the terminal took off. Hotels, apartment buildings, and skyscrapers sprang up along Park Avenue and 42nd Street. As the neighborhood prospered, so did Grand Central. In 1947, over 65 million people—the equivalent of 40 percent of the US population—traveled the rails via Grand Central Terminal. By the early 1950s, however, America had become a nation of suburbs and automobiles, and revenues from long-distance rail travel were plummeting. At the same time, the value of Midtown Manhattan real estate had risen dramatically. Preservationists became alarmed over talk of demolishing Grand Central Terminal and replacing it with an office tower.

On August 2, 1967, New York City's recently established Landmarks Preservation Commission designated Grand Central Terminal as a legally protected landmark. But the following year, the validity of the City's landmarks law was challenged in court. Litigation lasted nearly a decade. In 1978 the US Supreme Court upheld New York's law, leaving the terminal safe from the wrecking ball. But the story was not over; after decades of deferred maintenance, the building was crumbling.

Major repairs and improvements were made between 1983 and 1990, and in 1994 the Metropolitan Transportation Authority gained long-term control of the building and embarked on a comprehensive revitalization plan. Today Grand Central Terminal has been completely restored to its 1913 splendor and is a Midtown destination as much for its many restaurants, cocktail lounges, and specialty shops as for its role as a major transportation hub.

GRAND CENTRAL TERMINAL

Exterior of Grand Central Terminal, showing Mercury frieze.
View from Park Avenue South.

707 782 9000   WWW.POMEGRANATE.COM

Pomegranate

GRAND CENTRAL TERMINAL

Grand Central Terminal's Beaux-Arts interior measures
275 feet long by 120 feet wide, and the vaulted ceiling is
125 feet high.

707 782 9000   WWW.POMEGRANATE.COM

Pomegranate

GRAND CENTRAL TERMINAL

Entrance to Tracks 24–26, Main Concourse,
Grand Central Terminal

WWW.POMEGRANATE.COM

707 782 9000

Pomegranate

Image © MTA Arts for Transit

GRAND CENTRAL TERMINAL

Beaux-Arts lantern fixture, exterior, Grand Central Terminal

707 782 9000   WWW.POMEGRANATE.COM

Pomegranate

GRAND CENTRAL TERMINAL

Grand Central Terminal's Beaux-Arts interior measures
275 feet long by 120 feet wide, and the vaulted ceiling is
125 feet high.

707 782 9000   WWW.POMEGRANATE.COM

Pomegranate

Image © MTA Arts for Transit

GRAND CENTRAL TERMINAL

Entrance to Tracks 103–104, Lower Level, Grand Central
Terminal. Note the elaborately carved marble.

707 782 9000   WWW.POMEGRANATE.COM

Pomegranate

GRAND CENTRAL TERMINAL

The most widely recognized train-terminal room in the world, the Main Concourse of Grand Central Terminal sees 750,000 people pass through each day.

GRAND CENTRAL TERMINAL

Grand Central Terminal's arch windows are 60 feet high at each end.

707.782.9000   WWW.POMEGRANATE.COM

Pomegranate

GRAND CENTRAL TERMINAL

The information booth in the center of Grand Central
Terminal's Main Concourse is a popular rendezvous spot.
Topped with a four-faced clock, the circular marble-and-
brass pagoda holds a hidden spiral staircase leading to
another information booth on the Lower Level.

707.782.9000 WWW.POMEGRANATE.COM

Pomegranate

GRAND CENTRAL TERMINAL

The restrooms at Grand Central Terminal are among the
highest-rated public facilities in New York City.

707 782 9000   WWW.POMEGRANATE.COM

Pomegranate

GRAND CENTRAL TERMINAL

The most widely recognized train-terminal room in the world, the Main Concourse of Grand Central Terminal sees 750,000 people pass through each day.

WWW.POMEGRANATE.COM

707 782 9000

Pomegranate

GRAND CENTRAL TERMINAL

The Tiffany-designed clock centering the sculpture
Transportation atop Grand Central Terminal has a
circumference of 13 feet (4 meters).

707 782 9000 WWW.POMEGRANATE.COM

Pomegranate

GRAND CENTRAL TERMINAL

The sculpture *Transportation,* by French artist Jules-Alexis
Coutan, sits atop Grand Central Terminal. Mercury is flanked
by Minerva and Hercules. Carved out of Indiana limestone,
the group stands 50 feet high and 60 feet wide, weighs 1,500
tons, and surmounts a clock 13 feet in diameter.

707 782 9000   WWW.POMEGRANATE.COM

Pomegranate

GRAND CENTRAL TERMINAL

Exterior, Grand Central Terminal, facing north, c. 1945

707 782 9000   WWW.POMEGRANATE.COM

Pomegranate

GRAND CENTRAL TERMINAL

The sculpture *Transportation* sitting atop Grand Central Terminal features Mercury, the god of speed. This represents both the speed of commerce and the speed of trains.

707 782 9000   WWW.POMEGRANATE.COM

Pomegranate

GRAND CENTRAL TERMINAL

In December 1976, the National Register of Historic Places designated Grand Central Terminal as a National Historic Landmark.

707 782 9000   WWW.POMEGRANATE.COM

Pomegranate

GRAND CENTRAL TERMINAL

The four-faced clock atop the Main Concourse information booth is the most recognizable icon of Grand Central Terminal. Each face is made of opal, and the clock's value is estimated at between $10 million and $20 million.

707 782 9000   WWW.POMEGRANATE.COM

GRAND CENTRAL TERMINAL

The zodiac on Grand Central Terminal's Sky Ceiling is backwards, inspired by an era when artists depicted the heavens as they would be seen from outside the celestial sphere.

707 782 9000 WWW.POMEGRANATE.COM

Pomegranate

Image © MTA Arts for Transit

GRAND CENTRAL TERMINAL

The beautiful melon-shaped chandeliers on both sides of the
Main Concourse of Grand Central Terminal are plated with
nickel and gold and lit by LEDs.

707 782 9000   WWW.POMEGRANATE.COM

Pomegranate

Image © MTA Arts for Transit

GRAND CENTRAL TERMINAL

Architectural detail, copper-clad roof ridge,
Grand Central Terminal

707 782 9000   WWW.POMEGRANATE.COM

Pomegranate

GRAND CENTRAL TERMINAL

Roof of Grand Central Terminal, viewed from atop the
MetLife Building

707 782 9000   WWW.POMEGRANATE.COM

Pomegranate

GRAND CENTRAL TERMINAL

The sculpture *Transportation,* by French artist Jules-Alexis Coutan, sits atop Grand Central Terminal. Mercury is flanked by Minerva and Hercules. Carved out of Indiana limestone, the group stands 50 feet high and 60 feet wide, weighs 1,500 tons, and surmounts a clock 13 feet in diameter.

707 782 9000   WWW.POMEGRANATE.COM

Pomegranate

GRAND CENTRAL TERMINAL

Architectural detail, interior, Grand Central Terminal

707 782 9000 WWW.POMEGRANATE.COM

Pomegranate

GRAND CENTRAL TERMINAL

Grand Central Terminal officially opened to great fanfare at
12:01 AM on Sunday, February 2, 1913. More than 150,000
people visited the new terminal on its opening day.

707 782 9000   WWW.POMEGRANATE.COM

Pomegranate

GRAND CENTRAL TERMINAL

Exterior, Grand Central Terminal, winter

707 782 9000   WWW.POMEGRANATE.COM

Pomegranate

GRAND CENTRAL TERMINAL

One of the many Guastavino-tiled, vaulted ceilings inside
Grand Central Terminal

707 782 9000   WWW.POMEGRANATE.COM

Pomegranate

GRAND CENTRAL TERMINAL

Arching over the 80,000-square-foot Main Concourse of
Grand Central Terminal, the extraordinary Sky Ceiling
portrays the Mediterranean sky with October-to-March
constellations and 2,500 stars.

707 782 9000   WWW.POMEGRANATE.COM

Pomegranate

GRAND CENTRAL TERMINAL

In 1947, over 65 million people—the equivalent of 40 percent of the US population—traveled the rails via Grand Central Terminal. Pictured: Main Concourse

WWW.POMEGRANATE.COM

707 782 9000

Pomegranate

Image © MTA Arts for Transit

SELECTED POMEGRANATE BOOKS OF POSTCARDS ON ARCHITECTURE AND DESIGN

Please contact Pomegranate for more information about our many books of postcards.

While Grand Central Terminal stands today as one of New York City's most famous landmarks, it was by no means the first railroad station in New York City. In fact, the current structure was neither the first to claim the name "Grand Central" nor the first to occupy the busy intersection of 42nd and Park. Yet, the story of Grand Central Terminal illuminates much of the history of the city of New York; the growth and expansion of a vibrant metropolis is reflected in this unrivaled monument of civic architecture. In both historical and modern photographs, this book of postcards surveys the terminal's architectural details, both inside and out, and looks at the bustling life surrounding this cherished edifice.

MTA
OFFICIALLY LICENSED

CAT. # AA745 $10.95 US

Pomegranate

ISBN 978-0-7649-6333-9

7 17195 23965 7

9 780764 963339   51095

CONTAINS 28 OVERSIZED POSTCARDS